Sam Flores

Sam Flores

June 11, 1929 - July 25, 2011

A conversation

Chiringa Press
Seguin, Texas 2012

Cover photo: Sam Flores.
            B company 1st Battalion, 5th Marine, 1st Marine Division

Design: Michael Godeck

ISBN 978-1-61012-025-8
© 2012 Chiringa Press
chiringapress@gmail.com

In Gratitude

We would like to express our thanks to the Flores Family for allowing us to publish this written recollection by Mr. Flores as a contribution to the

Seguin Stories - Historias de Seguín Project.

Velia García Flores

César Javier Flores

Samuel James Flores

Leticia Flores

In Loving...

Presentation

The Seguin Stories - Historias de Seguín Project started a few years ago upon the initiative of Mr. Ramón Salazar and Mr. Edward Dávila, distinguished Hispanic business leaders and citizens of Seguin. They realized the importance of telling their story for future generations to have a good idea of their roots and an appreciation of the work done by their ancestors for the betterment of the community.

Dr. Ana María González, Associate Professor of Spanish at Texas Lutheran University, embraced this task and started working with her Spanish language students in order to reach two goals: improve their language skills and provide a service to the community.

Through this project, Dr. González has met relevant people and learned about their lives, struggles and accomplishments. She also came to understand that there was a name that constantly appeared in several of the projects related to the improvement of life conditions of the Hispanic community of Seguin: Mr. Sam Flores. She then decided to present a request directly to him and asked him to write his individual story. Mr. Flores gladly accepted and in the summer of 2010 he started his own narrative. Unfortunately, Mr. Flores' health condition rapidly deteriorated and he didn't have the opportunity to complete his objective. He passed away on July 25, 2011.

The present work symbolizes in part the life of an exceptional man with a great vision for his people, who was also involved in many different aspects of the social, cultural, political and economic life of Seguin. He is a role model for many and his legacy will continue through the work that his followers are able to undertake and achieve for the benefit of Seguin.

Ana María González

Sam Flores

- A conversation -

My parents José S. and Agustina came from Mexico. Both had the same last name, Flores. My mother's parents were Luciano and Adela Flores.

When my father came from Mexico he went to work on a farm where his uncle was working. The work included regular farm work and menial jobs that the property owner would assign his workers. In those days many people coming from Mexico were employed by Anglo property owners; who provided homes to the immigrants on their property. Many property owners would pay their workers with some crops such as corn, wheat, potatoes, beans, etc. Also, many workers were allowed to have some domestic animals such as cows, chickens, and hogs. While work was really hard workers were grateful to have a place to live for them and their families. Most workers did not pay rent for their homes. But their homes were considered as part of their benefits. While many workers did not receive regular pay during most of the year, property owners would arrange for them to have credit mostly at grocery stores. When the crops were harvested the owner would pay the workers debts and would pay them a percentage of the profits the money received for their crops.

Our homes were located on a large lot. Our home was small but our grandparents' (maternal grandparents) home was very nice, large and well kept. My grandparents kept chickens, a cow and some pigs. My grandfather would plant vegetables, in the large back yard of the property. In those days most Mexican-Americans were very poor. Their homes had outside toilets. The heat for cooking from wood stoves would also be used for heating during the winter. Our water for drinking, cooking, and other needs came from a well between our home and my grandparents' home.

My father and grandfather were good workers and providers. My grandfather was a "cedrero", a cedar worker. He would go to the woods and cut wood with an axe for eight or more hours per day. My father worked hard and diligently doing many jobs to support the family.

My brother Josué and I would enjoy riding in the back of a wagon which my grandfather had and would use often to carry a variety of things. My mother and grandmother were hard workers, because in those days life was hard. In those days my mother would iron and fold large amounts of clothes. After the clothes were washed the clothes were placed on a line to dry. When the clothes were dry they had to be taken down and folded. By now the family had grown: there was Francisca (Frances), Raquel (Rachel), Rebeca (Rebecca), Samuel (Sam), Josué (Joe), and Ester (Esther). This was about 1935. Thanks to God that my father and all of us were never sick, there were of course sometimes when there were minor illnesses and accidents but nothing major.

I actually do remember one occasion, when my sister Esther was about two years old and she fell off my grandparents' front porch. She cried a lot, but of course in those days Hispanic children would not or could not be taken to the doctors because the parents could not afford it. We had Tío Vicente who was a "curandero". He was called to see and treat Esther. Tío Vicente ordered some things for us to do and told us to make sure to follow the procedure he wanted us to do for Esther. This procedure allowed Esther's arm to heal. Today Esther has a slight bump where that accident happened.

Another occasion, according to my parents, was when I was about three years old. They indicated that I was very hyperactive. In those days many people would make their own toys. I was playing outside in the dirt and I found a can with white stuff. Thinking it was something to eat I took some of it and put in my mouth. The stuff that was in the can was something really bad; my mother said that I was fortunate that I did not swallow a lot of it. It was lye. The lye was all over my mouth and my tongue for a long time. I cried and cried because I had a lot of pain. I never went to the doctor, but I was treated by my mother instead and it helped a lot. I never went to a doctor or a dentist until I was seventeen when I joined the Marine Corps.

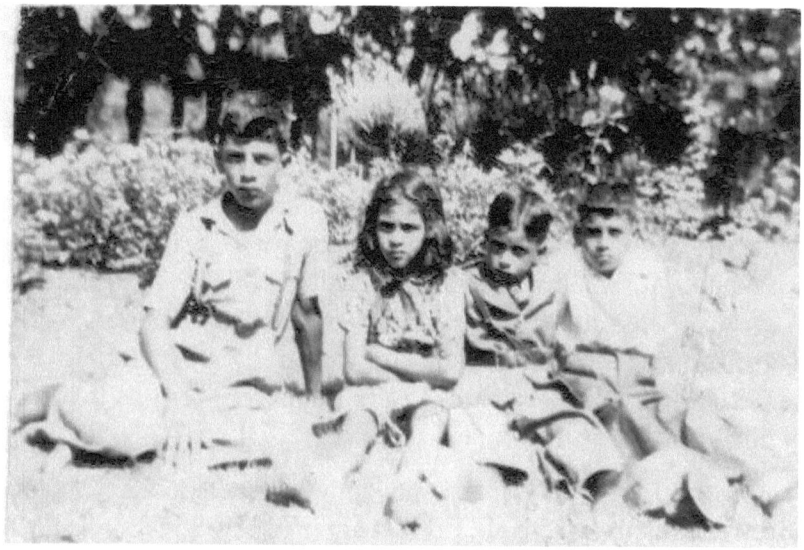

Sam, Esther, Daniel and Joe Flores.

Now around 1935 Frances, Rachel, Rebecca and I were in school. We went to an elementary school which was about two and a half block away from our home on Guadalupe St. in San Marcos, Texas. We all walked to school together. In those days there were no cafeterias or lunch school programs. So our mother would make us tacos and we would take them as our lunch to school. Many things came to my mind at that time like for most of the time we would go to school barefoot. That was acceptable for two reasons: many families could not afford shoes and it was an acceptable procedure for the school. Another thing was that none of us knew any English, we all spoke only Spanish. However there was a phrase that parents learned over the years, which was "be excused".

This meant that when the child raised his or her hand and said to the teacher "Ma'am, be excused" or maybe "Ma'am, may I be excused". This was understood, it was like a way to ask for permission to go outside to use the restroom. The toilets for students to use were outside. The desks and chairs were made out of wood. School was also segregated; there was segregation between Mexicans and Mexican-American children up to the 6th grade. I never understood why in elementary school Anglo students had the toilet facilities inside and we had them outside.

The school had ten teachers, Mr. Lumpkin, a fifth grade teacher was acting principal, and one of the teachers was Mrs. Murillo, who was also a Cuarterona. The janitor was a Black man named Freeman. Mr. Freeman was a good janitor. My best friend was Leo Cavazos. After stealing some peaches from a tree in an owner's yard, Leo ran across the street and was hit by a car and broke his leg. It crippled him. Leo and I were the best of friends before his family moved to California.

Around 1936 my parents moved, we moved about two blocks away on Austin Street, and now it is named LBJ Street in San Marcos, Texas. At the corner of Austin and LBJ St. the church faced Austin St. There were other things that were also located around these streets. We had electricity and a radio. The house we moved to was the Primera Iglesia Bautista's parsonage.

Unfortunately we were living in the time of the Great Depression of 1929. The whole nation was suffering from the great tragedy. Many of the banks were closed. Mexican-American men worked at menial jobs barely making a living. The government established an agency that would distribute some food to families who would apply for them. My father refused to apply for help so we would live by the salary that the church would pay him. Many of the church members would regularly give us vegetables such as potatoes, corn, beans, tomatoes, and eggs. At times they would also give him chickens and milk. Then one day, my father got a part time job as a cook at the San Marcos Academy. On one occasion, while using an electric meat cutter, he cut off two fingers from his left hand.

The community lived in segregated neighborhoods: Anglos, Blacks and Hispanics. The churches were also segregated. The Black and the Hispanic neighborhoods had gravel streets and during the summer weather dust would fly all over the place. Once a week a water truck from the city would pass by and water the streets to keep the dust down. As it got worse everyone did what they could do to help. Many people would have to go to town to get the stuff they needed. I didn't earn a lot of money but I made enough for my personal use shining shoes. Most of the boys didn't have much to do except play all day at the south side school playground which was right next to our home. We played mostly softball, football, and basketball. Many of us took up smoking. We started to smoke cigarettes, made from cedar posts which were used to hang wire fences.

There were very few things to do except play and hang around the house. The girls were even more limited. In our family the girls were limited to home, school, and church. My sisters were very involved with church work. They all also helped my mother around at home. While the economy was really bad because of the depression, my family and other families in our neighborhood still lived really happy. Women that lived in the neighborhood would help each other out. Whenever someone needed something whether it was sugar, coffee and other things they would all help each other out. My family always had frijoles which were beans. My grandmother made the best frijoles in the world. Around the age of nine and ten I liked to hang around my grandparents' and help my grandfather out or saw wood logs. After we finished cutting wood, my grandmother would always call us in for supper. Most of the time it was frijoles, which were homemade by her, she would also make fresh flour tortillas, and most of the time she would cook some type of meat called guiso. I really enjoyed these meals.

Our family continued to be involved with the church and their activities, and everything they would host. In about 1937 my mother started getting sick. Her symptoms were weakness and on some occasions she would faint. We all did what we could to make her feel better. She continued feeling ill but she still continued to care for us. Frances and Rachel, my two older sisters, were now old enough to help her do all of the house work. One morning in 1939 the family was still asleep. The three boys Joe, Daniel, and Sam were asleep on the living room floor. One morning my father woke us up crying and told us mother had died in her sleep. I still remember that horrible event. As my father finished telling us the story of that event I panicked and got up from the floor running outside of the house barefooted and crying loudly. I was ten years old. In those days, we the boys slept in our regular clothes. I ran fast crying around two blocks and then ran to my grandparents' home to tell them that mother had died. I was afraid to return home, I didn't want to believe that mother had passed away. This was the saddest day of my life... Two days later we had the wake and then we had the funeral service that was held at the church. We took mother and buried her in the cemetery in the small town of Martindale near San Marcos, Texas.

Now we were alone three boys and four girls, and with a father being a single parent. For several weeks all of us were in deep mourning. There were many changes that came along after the death of mother, school, work, and many other things. The following year Rachel quit school to take care of the house and basically served as our mother. Frances continued her studies and graduated from San Marcos high school in 1940. My father continued to work in his ministry as he had undertaken another job as a missionary for the San Marcos Baptist Association. He worked with the help of the local Baptist church. Father was a good worker and he did many different things dealing with farming around the area. He didn't want us to be alone and became concerned. He employed an elderly lady about seventy years old and she practically stayed with us all week. Her name was Chaguita. She did some limited work around the house and was mostly there to keep us company. Chaguita was partially blind.

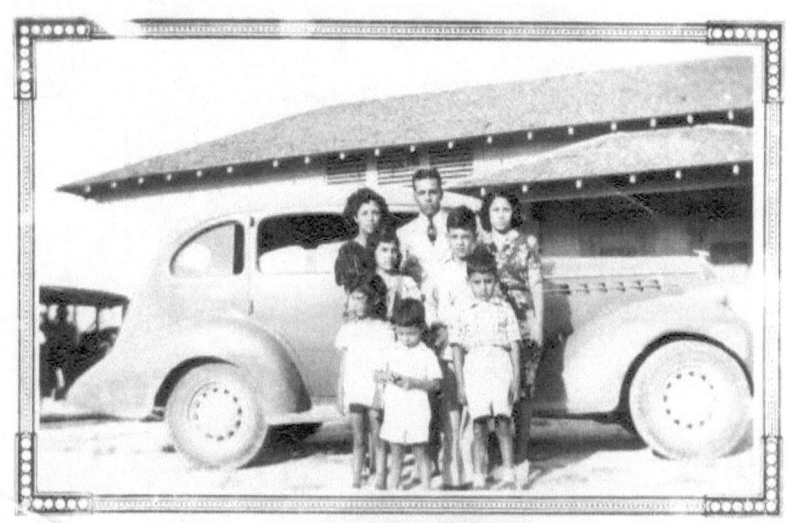

Flores Family after the death of their mother, Agustina Flores
July 16, 1939

About 1941 Frances, my older sister, got a job as a clerk typist and went to work for the U.S. Government in Washington, D.C. (Pentagon), New York City (Wallstreet), and St. Louis, Missouri. Two years later Rachel got married and left us: Rebecca, Esther, Joe, Daniel and me. We all continued in school. Rebecca was a good student and so were Esther and Daniel. Joe liked to work with mechanical things. In those days, homes with electricity had a fuse box and a fuse was needed for the electricity. When the fuse burned out, the electric lights would go out and the burned-out fuse had to be replaced. Joe somehow found out that if we didn't have money to buy a fuse, he would find a penny and place it where the burned-out fuse was and the electricity would be back on.

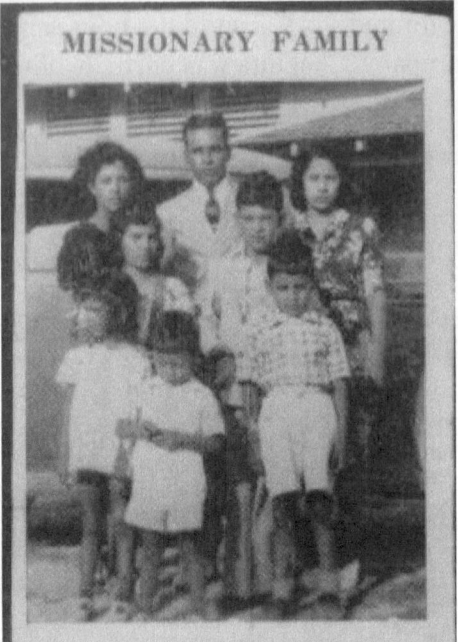

MISSIONARY FAMILY

Rev. J. S. Flores, Mexican missionary at San Marcos, Texas, and his
seven children, taken the day after
Mrs. Flores died, July 16. Brother
Flores is one of the Home Board's
best workers in Texas, and the people
of San Marcos love him very much,
according to Rev. J. L. Moye, field secretary on the Mexican field.

The death of Mrs. Flores in July
leaves this good worker without a
companion and the seven children
without a mother.

Article written in the Baptist Standard Newsletter around 1939.

In 1940 a year after mother died, several men from the San Marcos Baptist Academy, an exclusive private military school, came to talk to my father. They told father that the academy was offering to enroll all of us at the academy at no cost or expense to father. We would have the choice of enrolling at the academy and stay in the school dorms. Everything would be provided for us at no cost. Also the man said we could attend school there and remain living at home. Father discussed what the men had offered and asked us our opinion, we all mentioned that we were not interested in enrolling at the academy. We stayed at home and continued going to public schools.

When I was eleven years old I was baptized. Baptists are baptized by submersion into water by the minister. After baptism you became a regular member of the church with all the rights of a regular member. Since Southern Baptist churches are autonomous all decisions made for that church are made by the members of the church. Father baptized many of the church members in the San Marcos River. During the time father was the pastor at "La Primera Iglesia Bautista Mexicana" in San Marcos, Texas. He baptized over 600 persons. He baptized many others at the missions that he helped establish. They would regularly send father some money to help us.

After mother died someone took a picture of father with all of us. The picture appeared in the Baptist Standard, a national Baptist publication. The picture carried a story about father's ministry and also that mother had passed away. Sometime later father received a letter from an elderly Baptist couple in Virginia. The letter included their condolences for mother's death. After their concern and prayer for the family, they told father that they wanted to adopt him and the family. After careful consideration father agreed and we were adopted by mother and father Ely. The gracious couple came to San Marcos to meet us and visit us. After that we knew them as mother and father Ely. They would regularly send father some money to help us.

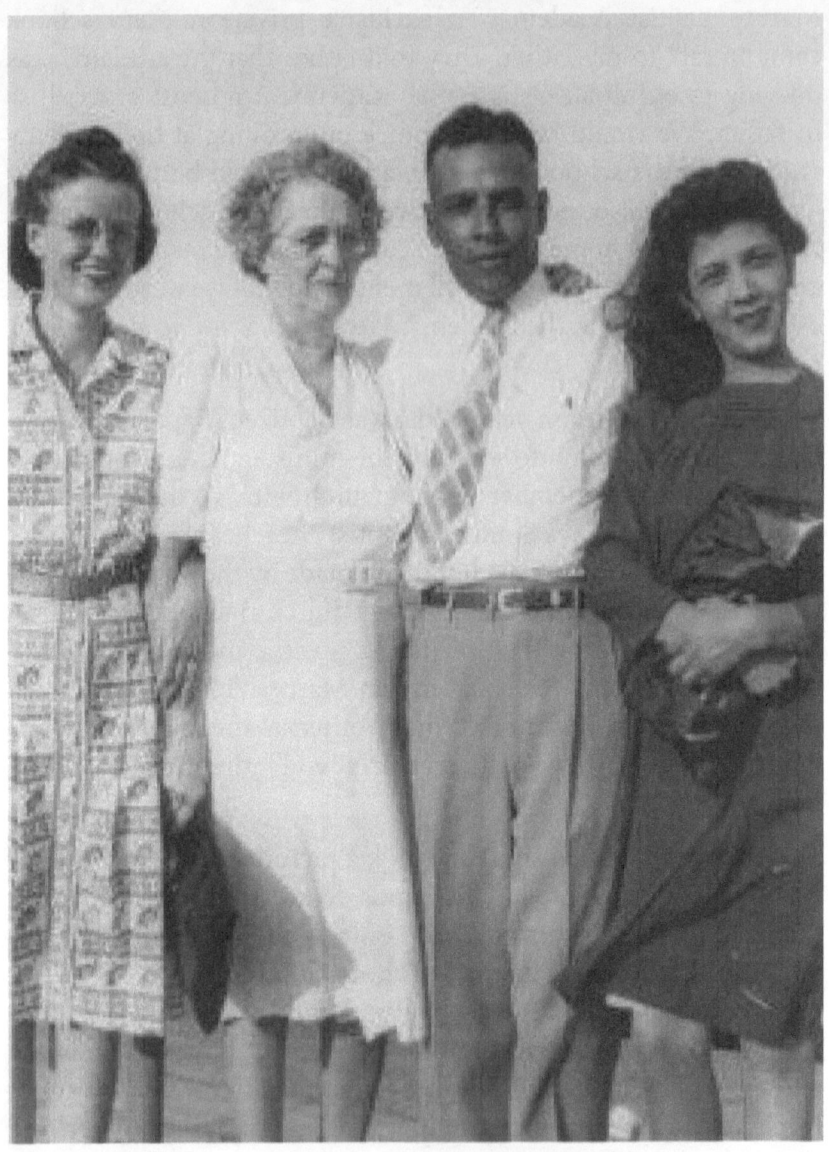

Mother Ely with her daughter, José S. Flores and daughter Frances
in Norfolk, Virginia.

In 1941, at the age of twelve, I and three other boys and three girls were double promoted to the 7th grade at mid-year. According to what we were told we were promoted because we were way ahead academically of the other 6th grade students at the South-side Elementary. Now those that were promoted had to attend San Marcos Junior High School which was about a mile and a half from my house. At the same time, both the junior high school and San Marcos High School were combined from grades 7-12 and were integrated. Black students had their own school. The principal, also district superintendent, was Fred Kederli.

The school was in a building next to Southwest Texas State Teachers College, in fact, the building was owned by the college at that time. The college must have had an enrollment of about 800 students at the most. Today it's known as Texas State University with an enrollment of over twenty five thousand.

I personally found the school to be very different and difficult. Most of the students were Anglo and the academics seemed more difficult. One of the things I found very difficult was the giving of oral book reports before the class, also you could sense that most teachers were partial to Anglo students and several teachers were out right discriminatory towards Hispanics. Another very prominent thing was that students associated only with their ethnic groups. The major improvement was that the building had all inside facilities such as restrooms and the school had a real nice cafeteria.

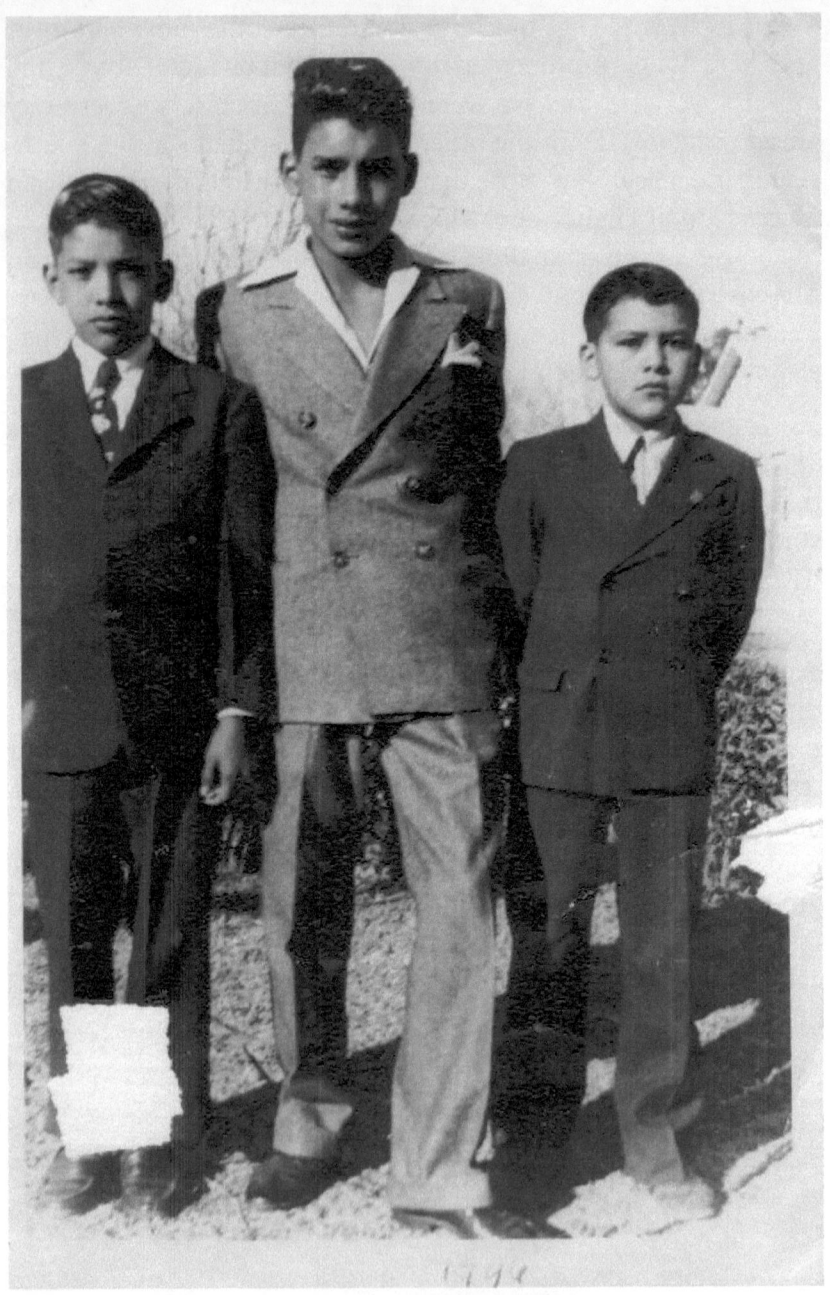

Daniel, Sam and their friend.

At the school students seemed to get along very well. Even at P.E. activities, the teams were made of all Anglos and all Mexican-Americans. In those days boxing was allowed in schools and no one could beat me in 7th grade. One day Coach Evans told me that I would be boxing a 10th grader named Jim Acree. Jim was about 6 to 8 inches taller than me and was large and known to be very strong. We started to box and it was a furious fight. The fight got so bad that finally the coach stopped it thinking that I or Acree would really get hurt. As the coach took my boxing gloves off he pulled me to the side and quietly told me "Flores it looks like the only one that can beat you is me" I said "Coach any time you are ready let me know".

I really liked and enjoyed sports. The school had a football team, the team was called "The Peanuts" the high school team were called the Rattlers. Looking back now I recall how the cheerleaders would yell "Peanuts, Peanuts, yea Peanuts" I made the first string on the team at right tackle at the end of the year the team members received something special like an award. It was a little gold covered football that was worn as a necklace and it was the most treasured award I received during my days at the junior high.

I was a fairly good student except when I got to the ninth grade because I had trouble with algebra. I was never able to pass algebra. In the ninth grade the school organized play nights where students could come and enjoy games and events. One play night we were playing a game of basketball, Anglos against Hispanics. During the game an argument developed between me and Bobby "Dizzy" Hall who was the quarterback for the football team. During the argument Bobby hit me hard and I hit him back so we got into a big fight. Miss Reed, one of the sponsors, came and stopped the fight. She blamed me for the fight and sent me home. I realized immediately that Bobby had ruptured my ear drum. Since then I always had to be careful not to get water inside my left ear because I got really bad ear infections. When I joined the Marine Corps in 1946 I never told them I had a busted ear drum because I would have not been accepted. In the Marine Corps whenever I had to go into the water or during the heavy noise from weapons I would pack my left ear tightly, with cotton. In Seguin in 1954 I got a really bad ear infection in my left ear. I went to see an ear specialist and I told him I had a ruptured eardrum but doctors had never been able to see it. He said that was no problem that he would find out in a minute if I had a busted drum. He looked at it and put some medicine into my ear. When he looked at the ear after putting the medicine he said that I did have a ruptured eardrum. But as soon as he put the medicine, I was able to feel it going through my ear tube burning badly: it went from my ear drum to my mouth. The doctor said you do have a problem with your ear drum.

During the early 1940's, my family was doing well, all of us were in school. My sister Frances was in Washington, D.C. and my sister Rachel had gotten married. Father continued his ministry as a pastor of the church and organizing missions around San Marcos. Father was highly respected and liked by everyone because he was always helping people. The Hispanic people knew him as "el hermano Flores" the Anglo people called him "Brother Joe."

At the age of 14, I started to not like going to school. I wanted to work. In those days there were no laws that required students to attend school. There was a family named Ríos from our church. The Ríos family would go to California every year to work as migrant workers. The Ríos family was made up of the father Ponciano, the mother Elvira, three daughters and five sons. Mr. Ríos made part of his family living by cutting wood with an electric saw and would sell it to people. Many people still used wood stoves. One day while cutting some wood, Mr. Ríos cut his hand and two fingers. He quickly asked someone to take him to the hospital. His hand healed after some time and he continued to do his work.

I was a very good friend of the two younger boys, Benjamin and Rogelio. All of the five brothers served in the armed forces: Arturo, Gustavo, and Noel in the Army and Benjamin and Rogelio served in the Marines Corps. During WWII Noel was wounded and Rogelio was killed. Benjamin was wounded during the Korean War.

Of the three girls, only the oldest, Oralia, attended school after the 6th grade and graduated from high school. She went to SWTSTC -Southwest Texas State Teachers College and earned herself a degree. She married Elías Rodríguez and moved to Seguin, Texas to teach at a school. She taught for a good number of years. Recently, the Seguin ISD school board decided to build a new school and named it after her: Oralia Rodríguez Elementary.

Because I didn't like school and liked working more, I asked Mr. Ríos if I could go with them to California. He said that I could if I would get my father's permission. I went to father and asked him if I could go to California with Mr. Ríos. I greatly admired my father because he always trusted me and my judgment. My father gave me permission to go. The Ríos family would go to California during the summer and return around November when we could re-enter school if we wanted to. In those days, many families traveled to Ohio, Michigan and other states to work in the fields.

Mr. Ríos had an old truck but he kept it in a really good condition. The back of the truck was covered with a very heavy canvas and they would put their belongings in the back. To me, this was a great adventure. Mr. Ríos would drive the truck all day. Just before night fall he would find a good place to stop and spend the night. When he stopped Mrs. Ríos would prepare supper. She would also prepare the food that we would be eating the next day during the day. She would cook breakfast before we would leave the next day. I greatly enjoyed this kind of life. I was amazed by many of the things I saw while driving. There were some dangerous places crossing the Rocky Mountains before reaching California. Brother Ríos was about five feet four inches tall. I am still amazed at the respect that all his family had for him.

When we reached California, brother Ríos already had made arrangements where we would be staying if a house was available. Most of the work we did was harvesting tomatoes, corn, peaches, apricots, plums, and a lot of other vegetables and fruits including grapes and watermelons.

As I said, I loved this kind of life. We worked hard all day normally having lunch at noon, mostly tacos and coffee. We came back from work until about 5 o'clock and Mrs. Ríos would already have a very good meal cooked for us to eat. Every meal included good beans and fresh made tortillas.

After the meal, the boys and I would talk or sometimes play games and listen to the radio. We normally went to bed early. Mr. Ríos had the truck bed fixed to where he could lift the bed. He also had a mosquito net installed all around the trunk. This would allow the cool nice breeze at night and we would sleep really well. If it rained, all we had to do was to drop the canvas all around the back of the truck.

We would get paid some good money, I recall that in San Marcos as a young boy you could earn 25 to 50 cents an hour. I remember making up to 35 dollars a day by just picking fruit or planting it, the job that we would normally do.

The fruit would come out like in small branches of grapes. People would be employed to do different things and to work and harvest different fruits and vegetables. Sometimes I would drive the truck with fruits to the canneries or to a place where fruit was put out to dry such as grapes. Where they worked they would also dry into raisins. Mr. Ríos was a very hard working man. In 1945 he built a small store on the corner of his property facing Austin St. a major street. The store was a tortilla factory that made fresh corn tortillas. It was probably one of the first in Texas. Several of his sons made the tortillas and sold them at the store. They would also package tortillas and distribute them to mostly small Mexican-American neighborhood stores. Today tortilla production both flour and corn is a major industry nationwide.

In 1946 "Chito" Villalpando a friend of mine that had gone to California with the Ríos family returned to San Marcos by train and I had also come back to enroll into school. This was about the time I started going to school, and I was very frustrated. I was seventeen years old and in the 10th grade by the beginning of

December. I decided to ask my father for permission to join the Marines. Even as a young boy I always thought about joining the Marines. In order for you to join, you had to be seventeen years of age and have your parents' permission. When I asked father again he always respected my ideas. He told me to think about it and if I was positive that I wanted to join the Marines then he would agree. He always prayed for me and asked God to take good care of me.

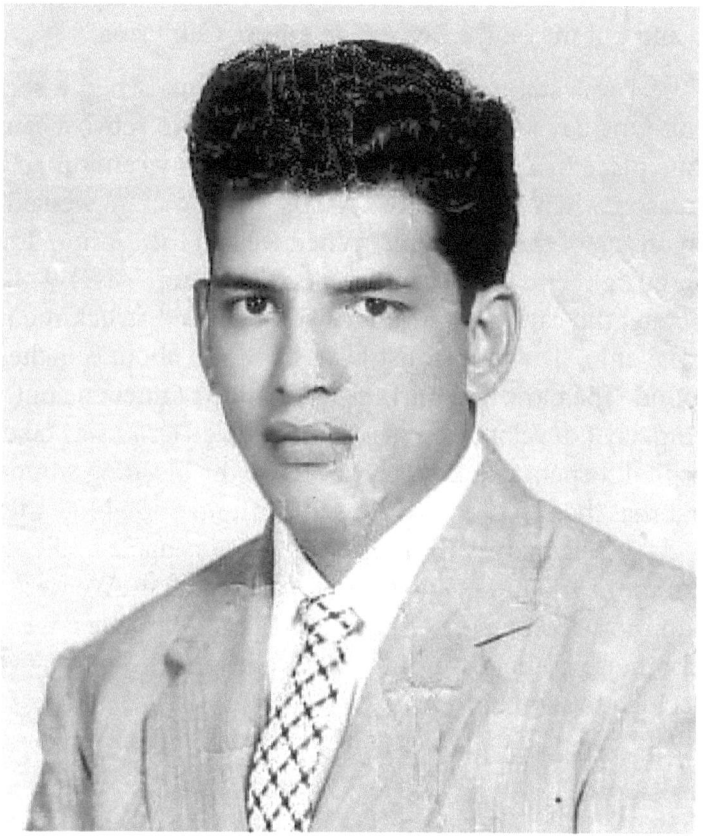

Sam Flores in his early years.

On December 5, 1946 I took a Greyhound bus to San Antonio and reported to the Marine Corps recruiting office. After a physical and psychological test I was found fit to enlist. I signed some papers and I was sworn in. I thought I would get a couple of days to go home. Instead, I was told that I would leave by bus in the morning for the Marine Corps recruiting depot in San Diego, California. I was driven to the Crockett Hotel right behind the Alamo where I would spend the night. The next day after breakfast a Marine came by in a staff car and took me to the Greyhound bus station and put me on the bus to San Diego, California.

While I was stationed at Barstow, California I had a serious accident. One day at work six men were asked to move a cannon from one place to another. We moved the heavy cannon and for some reason when we came to a large wooden crate we laid the cannon on top of the crate table. When we laid the cannon down I was on the light end of the cannon. As the cannon was laid on top of the crate, the cannon went like a sew-saw and struck me right under the chin. The blow must have lifted me about 3 inches off the ground. The blow had hurt me but it didn't knock me out. The following day I developed a massive nose bleed and I was taken to the hospital. I spent two days there before the bleeding stopped. I was told that the bleeding was caused by the cannon blow the day before. After several months in the Corps I was made a PFC and I was sent to the island of Guam in the Pacific Ocean. We were sent to a camp to become part of the First Marine Brigade. We were there for more combat training and were ready to go anywhere they decided to send us.

While there on the Island of Guam Island I was promoted to corporal and placed in charge of a 12 men squad. I took my duties very seriously. During our stay at Guam the services Army, Navy, Air Force, and Marine Corps decided to form a football league and compete against each other. In the Marine Corps during peace time you trained in the morning and you could join such teams for athletics.

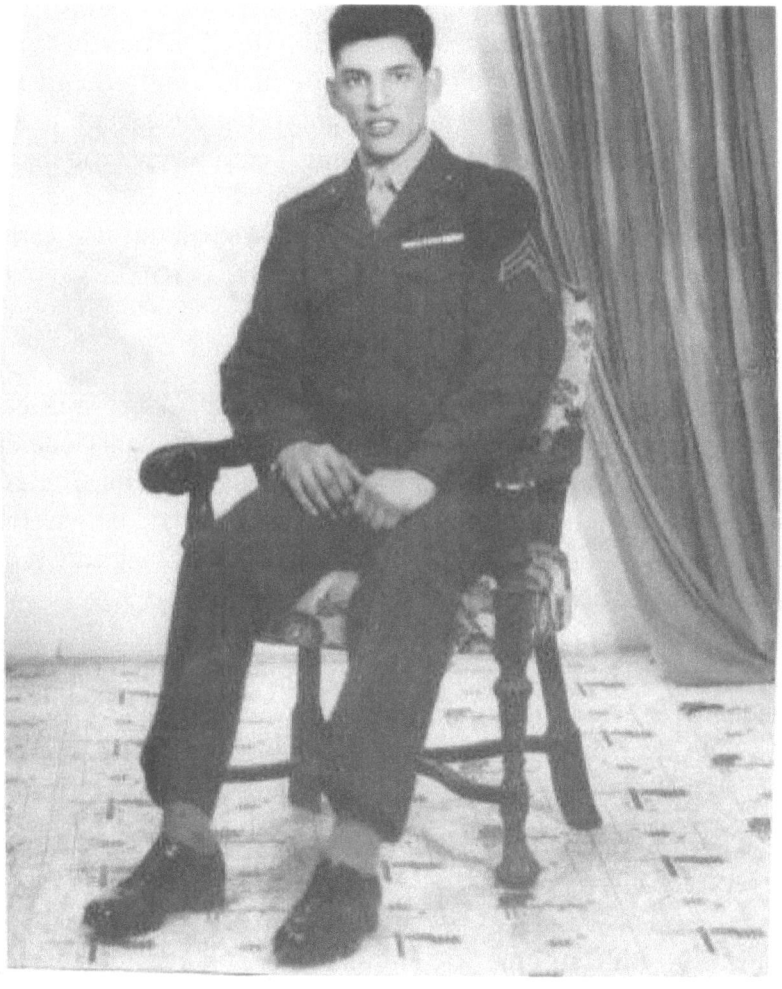

Sam Flores in his Marine Corps uniform.

Baseball, football and other sports were the ones we played. When they were organizing a football team I was interested; I had played a little football in high school. I must have weighed at the most about 150 pounds. I went to the captain, the company commander, to ask for his permission to try out for the team. He said "Flores, you are you crazy those guys that are trying out are mostly college players". I said "well I just need your permission to try out for the team". About three hundred men went to try out for the team. After extensive plays they decided on the 48 players that they wanted on the team. I found out I made first string. When I returned from the try outs I went straight to tell the captain that I had made the team. He said to me Flores I can't believe you made the team. After training in about three weeks we were scheduled to meet the team from the 20th Air Force. We had our first game and the score was 0-0. I was standing next to the coach (Lt. Colonel Walt) when I saw he was so emotional that he was shedding tears. The score ended 0-0.

During the Korean War and Vietnam War Colonel Walt became famous as a warrior and was promoted to Lieutenant General. At that time China was undergoing the civil war. The Chinese nationalists were fighting the Chinese communists. The government was very concerned that many Americans living in China were in danger because of the war. The First Marine Brigade was dispatched to China to oversee the evacuation of any Americans that wanted to leave because of the war. The First Marine Brigade was there for 3 months and got all of the Americans that wanted to leave China out safely. There was a lot of fighting in China. We had been stationed in Shanghai.

We left by ship and we went to Pearl Harbor where we stayed for several days, then went to the Panama Canal and stayed there several days in Panama City, and then went by ship to Camp Lejuene, North Carolina. The entire trip took about three weeks and we traveled half the distance around the world. At Camp Lejuene we continued our combat training and readiness. About two months after arriving at Camp Lejuene I was notified that

I was being promoted to sergeant. I was also notified that I had made the second highest score in the Marine Corps on the test for Sergeant which I had taken when we left Guam. The test score was based on all the Marines taking the test for Sergeant at that time.

The time at Lejuene passed quickly and soon I would complete my three year enlistment. On December 4, 1949, I was discharged. I was given the opportunity to enroll in the inactive reserve and keep my rank. Enlisting in the inactive reserve involved being re-called back into active duty in case of war or national emergency.

After discharge, I returned home to San Marcos, Texas. I and the entire family were extremely happy to be together again.

I enrolled in college in San Marcos, Southwest Texas State Teachers College, under the World War II GI Bill and they accepted me on the basis of having acquired a GED diploma while I was in the service. I was enrolled under the condition that I had to make passing grades. I managed to pass my studies and after the first semester I enrolled in the summer session of 1951. In the meantime the Korean War had broken out and I was recalled to active duty. At that time a Sergeant from the College ROTC came to see me and told me since I was a WWII veteran I was not required to be on recall if I would join the College ROTC. I told the sergeant that I appreciated the information but that I would keep my commitment to the Corps and return to active duty. By October of 1951, I was back in the Corps and I had not even been out of a service a full year. I was ordered to Camp Pendleton, California and received further combat training to report to the war in Korea. After several months of training and a brief visit home I with thousands of other Marines left for Korea in January of 1951.

We arrived in Korea as replacements, we disembarked from the ship placed in military trucks and handed off to the authorities. It was extremely cold and the American and Allied Forces had been driven all the way back to the south of the peninsula of South Korea. The following day we made it to the front in what was called Operation Killer. We arrived at our destination late in the evening.

It was freezing and raining with the snow on the ground; being so late that we were taken to a spot and told to wait there until morning. It became night and there I was standing on top of the snow, freezing and raining. I was so cold and hungry; I made an effort to open a can of pork and beans, I could not open the can because my hands and fingers were almost frozen. One could not sit down or even lie down. You just stood there like a wild animal and endured the punishment. As it continued to rain the snow started to melt and pretty soon I was standing in freezing water, all the way up to my waist. This was the most miserable night I had in Korea, and I thought if it's going to be like this I will never make it.

Back home in San Marcos everyone was fine. My father married. He married a lady named Concepcion Rivera who was a missionary that was working with children in our church. Frances and Rachel were married. Rebecca was also married and had a boy named Ricardo, whom we called "Cookie", and Esther my younger sister had married an Air Force soldier from Kentucky.

Joe, my younger brother, had enlisted in the Army and was in Alaska with an 88' aircraft unit. Daniel my younger brother was still in high school. Daniel was on the Varsity Football team and from news paper articles sent to me, he was an outstanding player.

I had been in Korea about three months and we, the Marines, were regularly involved in Minor fire fight with the North Koreans. Then on June 17, 1951 our company (B company 1st Battalion, 5th Marine, 1st Marine Division) was ordered to assault Hill 907. It was the highest peak called the Punch Bowl because it was part of a massive crater created by volcanoes many years ago. The hill was heavily fortified by Chinese and Korean troops. By now I was a platoon sergeant and second in commanding the first platoon made up a 60 men. As we climbed up we were met with a massive amount of enemy fire. The enemy had the advantage. They were on top of the hill looking down on us and they were in heavily fortified bunkers. We were involved in a fire fight for almost five hours and getting casualties and some killed in action. Finally it was getting dark and the battalion commanding officer ordered us to withdraw because he knew we were running low on ammunition and the enemy was in a well fortified bunker with possibly a lot of ammunition. This was the most dangerous battle that I was involved in my year in Korea. The following day more Marine Units were ordered to again assault Hill 907. The report we received was that the hill was deserted. This probably happened because the massive battle that had occurred the day before.

During my one year in Korea I had about six platoon leaders, and I was the officer in charge of the platoon. I, as the platoon sergeant, was second in command. As the platoon sergeant you were always assigned to be at the front of the platoon during combat assaults. This did not mean that you were very brave, but because you had the rank and you were first. During my time in Korea I was involved in four major campaigns and many small fire fights against North Korean and Chinese soldiers.

Of the six officers I had, one was named Baker. He was nick-named "Muzzle Blast Baker" because of his abusive behavior and language. One day while we were behind the frontline, I and some of my men, all Mexican–Americans, were right outside the tent of Lt. Baker. All of a sudden, he came out fuming and yelled at me, Sgt. Flores, "I want you and your men to stop speaking Spanish because I do not understand a word of it" he told me.

I said, "Sir, we have been speaking Spanish among ourselves ever since we got to Korea." He said, "That is fine but I am ordering you to stop it." Right after that I went to the Company Commander and told him what had happened. He said, "Flores, I know you and some of your men speak Spanish among yourselves and I don't see anything wrong with it. You keep on doing it, and I will speak to Lt. Baker." And that was the end of it. In the Corps, Mexican-American Marines were very clannish and we looked for other Mexican-American Marines to associate with. When I became platoon sergeant many Mexican-Americans asked for transfers to my platoon.

One of my men was Heron Farias, he was nicknamed "Chico". One day he received a letter that his mother was very sick and would probably die. He came to me and showed me the letter and said, "I would do anything if I could go see her in Kingsville, Texas." I said "*Chico*, go see the captain, the company commander and see if he would let you go." It was difficult we were right in the front lines. *Chico* went to see the captain and came back very sad and rejected. He told me that the captain had said no that it was not possible. I told *Chico* let me go see the Captain. I told the Captain that *Chico* was an exceptional Marine and I told him that I thought Farias should be allowed to go see his mother and then he could return after she had died or got well. I convinced the Captain that it was only human for him to allow Farias to go see his mother. I came and told *Chico*, "Get ready and go see your mother." A month later he returned back to the platoon. His mother had gotten well.

On one occasion when we were in the reserves and behind the lines I was in charge of the platoon because we did not have an officer. Out of the one year I was in Korea I was in charge of the platoon for about 4 months. One day I received a call from the captain and he said come down to the company headquarters, he said we have a replacement for your platoon leader. I came down from the hill to see the captain. He said Sgt. Flores this is Lt. Joe Holt your new platoon leader. The lieutenant said, "I will come by tomorrow to meet the men."

The next morning Lt. Holt arrived and I had already had called the platoon into formation. Lt. Holt spoke to them and introduced him as the new platoon leader. Then he told me to dismiss the platoon. Before he left he spoke to me and said, "Sergeant this is the dirtiest group of Marines I have ever seen. Have those men cleaned up and have them ready for inspection tomorrow. When he left I told the men what Lt. Holt had said. They did not appreciate it and quickly dubbed him Lt. "Mother" Holt. The next morning Lt. Holt arrived, and I had the men looking spic and span. The lieutenant looked very satisfied with the apparent change in the men's overall appearance. Holt came up the hill to assume command. He and I would share a bunker.

A few weeks later Lt. Holt received several very large packages. He opened them and they were full with all types of food and snacks. He said these packages were from his father. He said his father was vice-president of the Kraft Food Company. He told me to pass out the food to the men. He regularly received packages and everyone appreciated the goodies. One day the captain called for Lt. Holt to come down to his tent. An officer from the regiment had come down and told him that the general wanted Lt. Holt to go and have supper with him. The officer was to transport Lt. Holt to the General and transport him back. I thought to myself who is this guy that the general invites to have supper with. Apparently, Holt was well-known and had a lot of pull and influence from somewhere.

Holt had been there a month working with our platoon and was ordered to make a raid on an enemy position in front of our lines. Lt. Holt advised us of the assignment and the following day we left walking towards our objective. He was leading the platoon when he stepped on a flare that broke his leg. He never saw any action and was flown to Japan to be treated for his broken leg. As a non-commissioned officer you carry a lot of clout in the front lines where the fighting had stopped. It was very cold and the men would eat all kinds of garbage, like powdered, eggs, etc. They would eat out in the open together and eat from their metal gear and canteens. The officers were inside a tent which was very comfortable and warm. I couldn't believe what the officers ate. There were Marines waiting on the officer's breakfast. For breakfast, they had hot coffee, fresh eggs -anyway they wanted them, fresh bread toast, bacon and butter, and you could eat as much as you wanted. I could not believe they had fresh eggs and everything else. It was really an injustice how the enlisted men ate and the conditions they ate in.

I left the service in February of 1952. Several months later I received a letter from the U. S. Congress it was a letter from Joe Holt.

He left the Marines after healing from his broken leg, finished his tour of duty, ran for congress and was elected to represent the district around Van Nuys, California. He had written to see how I was doing and to let me know where he was at, The House of Representatives at Washington D. C.

When I arrived home in 1952, I was not able to enroll back in college. I decided to look for work, until such time I could en-roll for the summer session. The only job I was able to find was as a janitor at the Offices Club at the San Marcos Air Force Base, I had worked there several months when an old friend of mine Noel Ríos, who had two small boys asked me if I could take him and his family to Minnesota where his in-laws and the family were working as migrant workers. I had bought a car with money that I was paid after I was discharged from the Marines. I told Noel that I would take him and his family to Minnesota.

We arrived in Minnesota where the Gonzales family was. The family was made of two parents, two grown sons and five single girls, the youngest was about thirteen years old. Everyone worked except the mother who had to stay home and keep the house. I was amazed at how strong and hard the girls worked. Most of the work was very hard out in the open. The work was mostly harvesting all kinds of vegetables including sugar beets and potatoes. I liked the work in Minnesota and after talking to Mr. Gonzales I would stay there with them to work. He welcomed me and I stayed there with them and boarded with them, all while paying him for my keep. I was there about two months when I received a letter from my father telling me that I should consider returning home, and re-enrolling in college. He said your home is here and you have the WWII GI Bill and the Korean GI Billl, then he said the university is here in San Marcos and we live here, he concluded those are all big advantages.

I always had respect for my father's recommendation, so I decided to return back to San Marcos to enroll in school. I left Minnesota one morning about 4:30 am, on a distance that was

1,200 miles. When I left I decided to drive straight without stopping only to refuel and pick up a snack. I drove all that day and kept driving the following day. I wanted to know how long it would take me to get home. It seemed that the next day I started to get tired and sleepy but I took a lot of "No Doze," to keep from sleeping. When I arrived in Texas about twelve midnight I was truly exhausted, but I kept on driving till about 1:00 in the morning. I arrived at Temple, Texas about 100 miles from home. At that time a big storm with lots of rain and wind started. It was one of the worst storms to ever hit Texas. I could hardly see where I was driving. I finally arrived in Austin about 30 miles from home and the rain was pouring with very high winds.

There was no way that I could find my way through Austin in the condition I was in. The only thing I could see was the dome of the State Capitol. I knew that Congress Avenue was right in front of the Capitol and drove in that way. I kept my sight on the capitol dome and I proceeded to go on different streets including alleys until I arrived in front of the capital and hit Congress Avenue going south to San Marcos 30 miles away. The storm was still raging and raining so hard that you could hardly see and then in my poor physical state; I was confused and thought that I was lost. In 1952 there was hardly any traffic on the highway. When I was ready to give up and confused my car headlights saw a sign that said Tenorio Grocery. Then I realized and remembered that was the name of a store in Kyle, Texas about seven miles from home. I went slowly to San Marcos. I arrived home about 5 am fully exhausted. I got home and someone opened the door and I barged in didn't say anything and went right to bed. The storm that I had driven through was one of the worst in the state of Texas, it caused heavy and extensive flooding all over the state. I thanked God for getting me home in spite of the long journey and driving through the massive storm.

The following second summer session of 1952 I enrolled again at Southwest Texas State Teachers College. President Lyndon B. Johnson attended and graduated from this college.

As always I was very active in the church. La Primera Iglesia Bautista Mexicana. The congregation had a new church. In 1950 the church sold its property to the San Marcos Independent School District. The property sold was adjacent to the Southside Elementary School. With the money from the sale of the property the congregation bought a large old home and its property on the corner of Guadalupe Street and Grove Street. Guadalupe Street was and still is one of the major streets in San Marcos. Today the church has a congregation of about 251 members. Most of the preaching now is in English.

Our family remained pretty stable: living at home was father, his wife Conception, Daniel my youngest brother, and Rebecca my sister (who had married and now divorced), with his two small boys -Robert "Bobby" and Richard "Cookie" Guerrero, and me. Daniel was still in high school. Joe was in the Army and Frances, Esther and Rachel were married. We lived in the parsonage that the church built next to the church. Frances had married Vincent Patlán, a WWII veteran. He graduated from Southwest Texas and he moved to Seguin where he started teaching school. They had one daughter, Thalia Marie. Rachel married Henry Renteria and they moved to San Antonio. Esther married Lonnie Bruce, an air man, and they moved to San Antonio where he was stationed.

I continued my studies at school, the more I attended the more I enjoyed school. I had a lot of friends, many from San Marcos and many in college that came from various cultures in Texas. It was still the social trend that most of all my friends were Hispanic. I was an average student. I believe I could do a lot better if I studied more but I was happy with just making passing grades.

In early 1953 I was director of the church's morning preaching service on Sunday. I had the position of Master of Ceremonies before the morning sermon, it included leading the singing. While at the pulpit I noticed that my sister Frances, who lived in Seguin, was accompanied by a beautiful young woman. They had come for the morning service and after the service was over I went to talk to

Frances and she introduced me to her friend. Frances said she is Velia Garcia and that they worked together. Frances worked at the Palace Theater in Seguin as a ticket cashier and Velia worked in the office as a secretary. We spoke briefly and then they left for lunch at a local restaurant. Before they left I told Frances to invite Velia to come again to the church. They returned the following Sunday. After the service I invited Velia to have lunch with me. She agreed and went to a nice Mexican Restaurant named Alex's Cafe. During lunch as we became more acquainted I asked her if I could see her again, which again I was surprised that she said yes. I started going to Seguin to see her and most of the time we went to the movies and then we could go out for a snack or for dinner.

After several times meeting with her she said she wanted me to go to her home and meet her parents. I said I appreciated the invitation. The following week I went to her home and she introduced me to her mother Elvira, they called her "Lilly" and her father Bartolo Garcia. They welcomed me and were very cordial. They invited me to stay for dinner which I did. There after we met regularly and several months later I asked her if she would be my girlfriend. Again she agreed, several months later I asked her if she would marry me. She said she would but she would have to speak to her parents. A week later she told me that her parents had agreed. She was their only daughter and they were very protective of her. I planned to meet with her parents to get their permission for me to marry her. After a discussion to know me better and explain my plans for the future they agreed for us to be married. We set the day for our marriage on December 20, 1953.

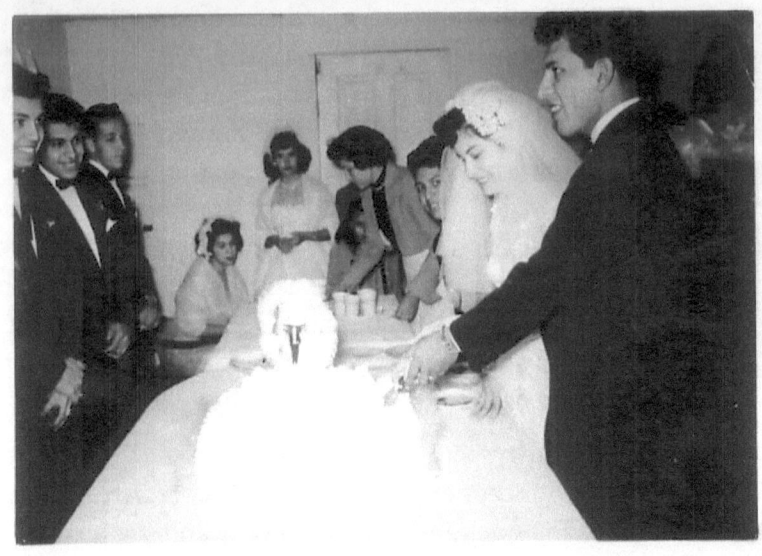

Sam and Velia's wedding day December 20, 1953
La Trinidad Methodist Church in Seguin, Texas

I was still a student in college but several months before our marriage I rented a home in San Marcos, I bought new furniture on credit. I had everything ready for us to move in after our marriage. About a month before our marriage, Adam Galaviz, my wife's cousin, told Velia that a man who had been her friend was very jealous because she broke up with him. The man told Adam that on our wedding day he would go to the wedding and kill me. Concerned about the threat we contacted the Guadalupe County Sheriff Phil Medlin who after explaining the situation told us that he would escort us to the wedding, and that he and his deputies would be outside the church to keep an eye out for the man. Velia had given him a description of the man.

On December 20, 1953 we were married at La Trinidad Methodist Church in Seguin, Texas with the Reverend Eugenio Vidaurri officiating. After the church wedding Phil Medlin escorted us back to my wife's house where we hosted a small reception. Everything went through without an incident that night. I borrowed my father's car and Velia and I went to Austin overnight for our honeymoon. We returned the following day and went to our home which I had rented. For the first several months Velia was at home as a house wife financially we were barely making it. We were living on the small subsistence that the government under the GI Bill was providing. She said she needed to work to help out. She managed to find a job in Seguin in the dental office of Dr. Freddie Sagabiel, a dentist. She would commute to Seguin by Greyhound bus and return to San Marcos in the afternoon, Velia and I were very happy. We didn't socialize much. Our life involved mostly my school and her work, attending church, the Iglesia Bautista Mexicana on Sunday morning and evening and on Wednesday night. Her parents and some of her friends and cousins from Seguin visited us often.

On Christmas Eve 1954 I borrowed my father's car and Velia and I invited Arturo Garcia and his wife Elsie. Arturo was a childhood friend of mine who had also served with the Marines in Korea. They had met in Honolulu, Hawaii and had married and he brought her with him to San Marcos. The Christmas Eve was mildly cold, and, misting. I always liked days like this. We drove around San Marcos enjoying the cruise with the radio playing Christmas music and the car heater on.

I told Arturo let's go to Martindale a small town south of San Marcos. It is a nice little town next to the San Marcos River. On our way back to San Marcos we came to a bridge over the Blanco River that led to the Gary Air Force Base from San Marcos, it carried a lot of traffic. As we came to the bridge I noticed that a car had stalled right at the entrance to the bridge and a man standing next to the car was obstructing traffic going north to San Marcos. I stopped my car right behind the stalled car. I put on the emergency lights on and told Arturo to get out so we could help the man get the car out of the way. We asked the man if we could help push the car off the bridge. The man got into the car and Arturo and I started to push the car. The cars that were coming south across the bridge started to slow down to allow us to pass. The first car coming south was apparently attempting to stop and put on the breaks. Because the ground was wet and misting, the second car behind the first one also attempted to break, but due to the wet ground the car skidded and struck the first car. As it hit the car the front car exploded and caught fire. It reminded of me when a whole box of matches goes off spontaneously I never saw anything like that not even in combat in Korea. As soon as I saw this happening, I ran to the burning car to see what I could do to get the occupants out. Velia, Arturo and Elsie just stood there in shock and Velia screaming at me to get away from the burning vehicle. I saw an elderly couple a man who was driving and a woman on the passenger's side. The couple looked about sixty five years old. In the back seat was a young man who looked about eighteen. They couldn't get out because for some reason the doors to the car were jammed.

I still remember the expression on their faces as they struck the windshield with their fist. The expression on their faces reminded me of a scared deer about to be killed. I got to the car but I couldn't open the car door. I had nothing in hand that I could use to break the car windows. By now a great number of cars had stopped and hundreds of people stopped and hundreds of them looking but no one dared to get near the burning car to help me. The people in the car were apparently returning from hunting and had ammunition in the trunk of the car. All of a sudden the bullets in the truck began to explode because of the fire and heat. Then people started yelling, and I continued to kick out the car doors and pull on the car handles but still I could not open the door. The couple and the boy in the car continued to cry and scream but nothing worked. I was ready to give up but I took my coat off and wrapped it around my right elbow and then with all my might with my back against the car driver side door. I cocked my right arm and hit the windshield which finally broke the car window. I was then able to get my arms into the car through the broken glass, and opened the door and got the passengers out before the car finally exploded again. After the whole ordeal I was exhausted. Velia came running to me very mad for risking my life. She was mad but embraced me and was happy that I wasn't hurt.

After the event I became somewhat frightened. I credit God and my combat training for acting as I did and saving those peoples' lives. Back in the car I said let's go to a restaurant and get something to eat, and we went to Carson's Café. I ordered a hot cup of chocolate and a large piece of coconut pie. It had been an interesting Christmas Eve and I felt pretty good.

On May 9th, 1955 I became a candidate for graduation from Southwest Texas State Teachers College. I had earned a Bachelor's of Science degree in Education with a minor in Art and Science. I had completed college in three years going full time including all the summer sessions. I had done very well as an average student. During the three years I had only failed a course in geography and made a D in elementary math. Most of my grades were C's with some B's but not one single A.

My wife, her family and I attended the graduation exercises at Evans Auditorium on the SWTSTC campus. I was happy and excited and looking forward to the future, and getting a job teaching. I just started to look for a job in Seguin and we made it back to my wife's hometown. I went to Seguin ISD and administrative offices and inquired about a job. I filled out an application and I was directed to Juan Seguin Elementary school. A fully segregated school from grades 1-6, Seguin ISD was the first district in the state to establish a totally segregated school. The school was called the Mexican School. A that time the state was allowed this type of setting; I went to see the principal and was told there were no vacancies. This is when I found out that Seguin School District did not employ Hispanic teachers for any of the schools except Juan Seguin. Now when I think about it, it makes me angry; but in those days we just accepted things like that. I should have sued Seguin ISD.

Discrimination was rampant in Seguin against Blacks and Hispanics. The Blacks were still totally segregated. All the elementary

Black students were enrolled at Lizzie M. Burgess Elementary; all the Black students were enrolled at Ball High school. All the teachers, and administrators, and support staff were Black. So pronounced did racism exist here in Seguin that the city kept people segregated. They had built a swimming pool for the Hispanics next to Juan Seguin School, a swimming pool for the Blacks at Ball High School, and the Anglos could use Starcke Park swimming pool. Restaurants would not allow Blacks to eat there. If you were Black you had to go through the restaurant's kitchen to buy your food and take it with you.

What a disgrace, Hispanics could eat at some restaurants but others still would not serve Mexicans. Vincent Patlán, my brother-in-law (married to my sister Frances) was now working in Seguin ISD as a Truant officer. When he just came to Seguin he went to one restaurant where he was denied service. Vincent was a WWII Army veteran that had been wounded and was no push over. He went to the American GI Forum organized by Dr. Héctor García from Corpus Christi, to help Hispanic Veterans. Vincent made a major complaint, the GI Forum got involved greatly condemning the practice of the restaurants and demanded that the restaurant open the restaurant to the Hispanics. In those days there were no laws requiring restaurants to serve all citizens. Vincent took his complaint to the media and generally created a lot of hell. The restaurant started to serve the Hispanics.

Seguin and the neighborhoods were all segregated. If you were Hispanic or Black you could not buy a home in most Anglo neighborhoods. Most Blacks and Hispanics were employed in menial jobs. There was rampant poverty and most of the minorities lived in substandard homes which mostly had electricity and running water but most homes had outside toilets. Seguin had 22 miles of gravel streets, all of them in the minority neighborhoods. For example, as far as a professional people, few Blacks and Hispanics were public school teachers. There was only one Black doctor, Dr. Friday. There were no Black lawyers or Hispanic dentists. There were only a few very small businesses such as little grocery stores. Anglo barbershops would cut hair for Hispanics and Blacks.

After I could get a job in Seguin I knew a friend of mine Rudy Aguirre who had been my scout master. He encouraged me to apply for a job in San Antonio Harlandale ISD where he and his wife were teaching. One day I decided to go to Harlandale ISD and apply for a job. I met with the superintendent Dillard Collum. After the interview he offered me a job in the 5th grade at Southcross Junior High a school with 1,200 students from grades 5-9. In August of 1955 my wife and I moved to San Antonio. I rented a house and started to lease. In 1955 Daniel, my youngest brother, graduated from school and for Joe my other brother next to me had been discharged from the Army. Daniel initially enrolled at Howard Payne University hoping to become a minister. After a semester there, he decided to join the Marine Corps because while in the Army, Joe had received a letter of commendation. The letter and certificate indicated that he had designed and built a bore sighting tool 88 mm for the aircraft guns. The citation stated that for years, army engineers had attempted to develop such a tool but had never been able to do so. Joe had designed and built the instrument. I always told Joe that he should have waited until after his discharged and then sell the bore sighting tool to the Army. I told him that he could have made a pile of money. Joe went to school for mechanics under the GI Bill. He graduated, got a job with Red Simon Ford in San Marcos and worked there for thirty two years, at the same time he also got married.

I had a car that my in-laws had given to us. It was an older Chevrolet but it ran well and was in good condition. As a teacher I was assigned to teach a self contained 5th grade class with an enrollment of 45 students. The only period I didn't meet with them was the P.E. class. The rooms were small and did not have an air conditioner. I was assigned room 11 across from the principal's office. The principal's name was Doug Sheldy. I was real interested in doing my job. The class was about 95% Hispanic and 5% Anglo. I taught all subjects including music. I found the students to be respectful and very dedicated to the school work. Most of them were on grade level. Teachers had a lunch period off and one hour period to be used for preparation and other class work. Most teachers used the period for resting in the teachers' lounge or talking to fellow teachers. There was a teachers' lounge for the men and one for the ladies.

Because I really cared for my students and wanted to do a better job, I used the preparation period to visit the homes of every student assigned to me. I met the parents and introduced myself as their child's teacher. Parents were surprised to see me there and told me that the teachers never visited their homes. By the end of the first month I had visited every home. The principal was very impressed and told me that he never had a teacher to do that. I don't want to sound presumptuous, but I was a good teacher. There were eight fifth grade classes, and my class was most of the time ahead of the other fifth graders, in daily attendance in academics and athletic competition. At the end of the first year, Doug Sheldy left to be an administrator in another school in the district. The man replacing him was Howard "Bull" Harris and he had been a high school football coach.

During that time new laws were passed that public schools would provide classes and teachers to teach special education to special needs students. One day, Mr. Harris called me and told me that he had to implement some classes for Special Education students. He told me and said I was his best teacher and wanted for me to consider teaching one of those classes. I said Mr. Harris I work here and you tell me what you want me to do. He assigned me to teach a class of mentally retarded students. I was involved in one controversy with Mr. Harris. The school was having a school wide declamation contest. I had a student that was very sharp named Tomás and I encouraged him to compete in the contest. I assigned Tomás to learn verbatim the Gettysburg Address. The contest was held several weeks later. After the judges finished then they reviewed and determined that Tomás had taken the first place.

Several teachers complained to Mr. Harris and said that Tomás shouldn't get the first place trophy, because he was in special education. Mr. Harris conceded, and when I found out I went to see him and told him that Tomás competed with regular education students. After Mr. Harris saw that I was getting assertive and demanding, he agreed with me and Tomás received the first place trophy.

I was always very involved with helping everywhere. Discipline of students was a major concern. There was an active gang in the community called the Circle Gang and some group of students many in the 8th and 9th grades were members of the gang. In the school most students were orderly and well behaved. I would say that about 3 of our students had discipline problems. During my days at Southcross, I took two loaded guns from students and also several knives.

My starting teaching salary was $2,805 for 9 months which equaled 172 school days. This was the state's beginning teachers' salary. In those days if you were married, you had to have a part time job. While at Southcross a veteran's administrator had hired me to teach two veterans one in Seguin, and one in New Braunfels, teaching them leather work and silver work for rehabilitation. They were both disabled. I had also gotten a job with the Harlandale district taking tickets at Friday night football games.

In 1956 after starting my second year teaching school, my youngest son Cesar was born. We continued to live in San Antonio. But because the house rents were high, we decided to move to Seguin and live with my in-laws and I would commute to San Antonio from Seguin. I did that for thirty five years.

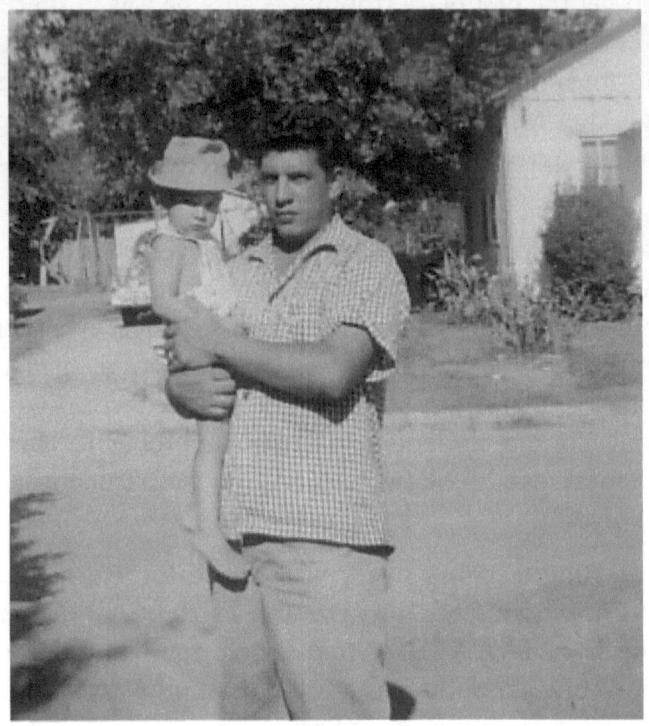

Sam with baby Flores

In 1964 I was assigned to a new program for older special education students. The school was in some old barracks purchased from the military. The plan here was to teach special education students both boy and girls vocational skills to make a living. We organized a curriculum with six vocational skills. There were shops teaching wood work, food services, bricklaying, gardening, and homemaking. We were very fortunate that we were able to get a lot of help getting equipment needed from the Texas Rehabilitation Commission. After a year or more, the students having mastered their field of training, we made an agreement with Goodwill Industries which had a large facility in the Harlandale area. At Goodwill the student was then assigned to different work stations to learn other skills such as arriving to work on time and learning to work with supervision. After the students learned those skills, by this time students were 17, 18 and 19 years old. At that time with the Texas Rehabilitation Commission, we again would place students for training in restaurants, hospitals, mechanic shops, and beauty schools. We even had some students training at Kelly Air Force Base. Students did not receive a salary while training, but when they finished training then we found jobs for them. Then they were employed and earned a salary. The Texas Rehabilitation Commission would pay for their training, and any tools needed, also for transportation to training to get to training and get back home. I was called a vocational adjustment coordinator. One time a student named Don started working as a janitor at the post office. I took Don home and I told his parents where he would be working and how much he would earn. The father hearing this said that was more than what he was making. Don's parents were very happy and excited.

After four years at Stinson, I was assigned a vice-principal position at Southcross Junior High. I was vice-principal and after two years, in 1970, I was assigned as vice-principal at Harlandale High School. The school had a principal and four vice-principals. The superintendent told me that I was second in command.

Harlandale High School was a good school. It was housed in very small facilities with an enrollment of 2,800 students. Sometimes we had study halls with over 200 students because there were not enough classrooms to assign them to. Across the street from Harlandale High there was a housing unit for low income families, a block down was a small shopping area where many students would go during the lunch period. We had an open campus. There was a time of major social change and also illicit drugs started to appear in schools.

Harlandale ISD was then about 85% Hispanic. During my four years at Harlandale I noticed that there was not one Hispanic principal or vice-principal in the Harlandale ISD. I called for a meeting with the superintendent Mr. John Gonder, who was a very nice person. After greetings I told Mr. Gonder that I came with a concern. I told Mr. Gonder that the district was about 85% Hispanic and yet it did not have a single vice-principal or Hispanic principal. I told Mr. Gonder I am not looking for a principal's job. Mr. Gonder was pensive for a moment and then he told me that I was right, and assured me that he would give the problem his attention.

The following year he appointed the first two Hispanic principals. Eddie Paredes at Stonewall Elementary and Emeterio Pérez at Southern Junior High. Later there were more appointed to jobs as administrators.

In the 1960's most of the things at my home and my father's were going well. My sister Rebecca passed away and left her two sons Robert and Richard with my father and stepmother. Richard was about fifteen years old and Robert about thirteen. Daniel my youngest brother had served four years in the Marines doing embassy duty. He had married Dorothy Arnett who was then a secretary to Abe Fortas before he became a Supreme Court Justice. Daniel had been discharged from the Marine Corps working part time for the state department and attending Washington University in D.C. He got his degree and joined the state department. Actually, I found out many years later that it was the CIA he worked for thirty two years.

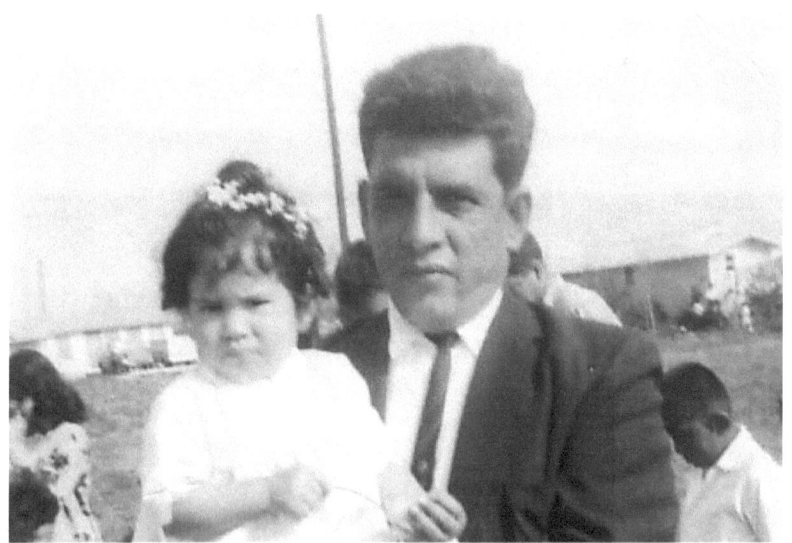

Sam with daughter Leticia.

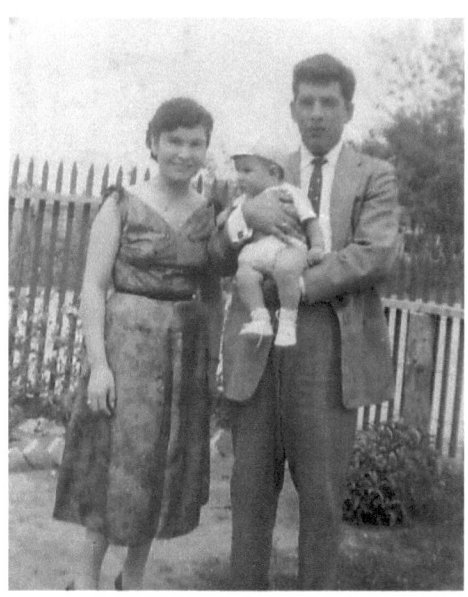

Velia, Sam and one of their boys.

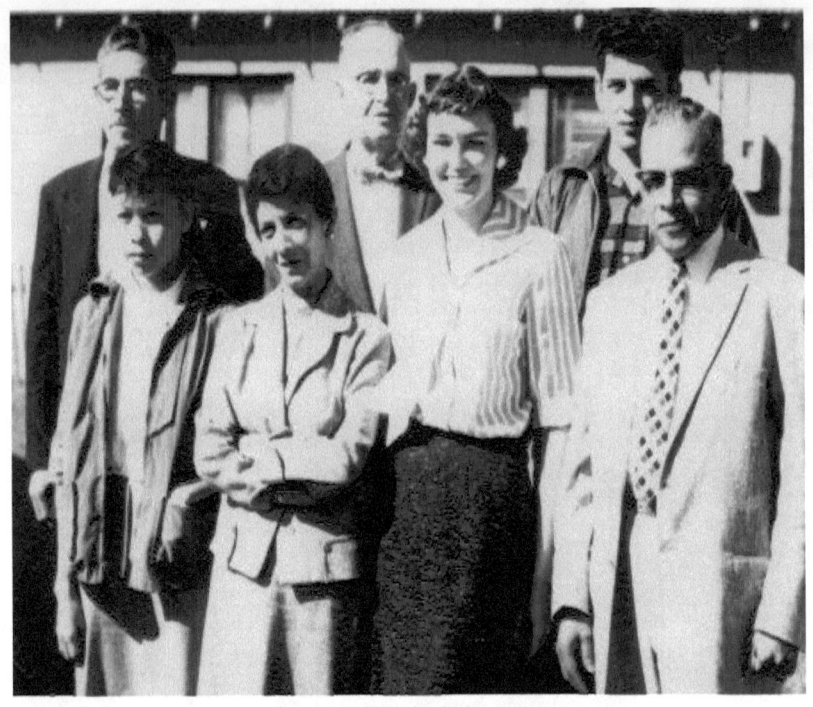

José S. Flores with members of his congregation and members from the First Baptist Church.

Front row: Flora Belmarez, Francisca (Frances) Flores Patlán, Ms. Collins, Reverend José S. Flores. Back row: Bartolo García (father-in-law of Sam Flores), Brother Sam Chrisco and Sam Flores.

(The photo was taken in the front of the Baptist Mission Church, located on Collins St.)

In 1963 Cesar, my oldest son, was ready to start school. The schools in Seguin were zoned and Cesar was assigned to Juan Seguin Elementary, a Mexican-American segregated school. The zone for Seguin passed right in front of my house on Chapman Street about 2 miles from Juan Seguin. I never thought much of the school being segregated but there was an elementary school, Weinert Elementary School, that was about a half mile from home. I told my wife that we would try to get him enrolled at Weinert and I went to see the superintendent A.J. Briesemeister. I told Mr. Briesemeister that I wanted to get a transfer for Cesar to attend Weinert Elementary. The superintendent said that would not be possible and students must attend the school in the school zone that they are assigned to. I thanked him and left. Some weeks later I found out that some Anglo students in the Juan Seguin School zone were given transfers to other schools in the district. I was very upset and angry and decided to go back to see the superintendent.

When I arrived, I told the superintendent's secretary that I needed to see him. She went to his office and asked him to give me a letter stating why my son could not attend Weinert School. He asked me why I wanted the letter and I told him that I knew that the district was giving transfers to other schools in the district to Anglo students that lived in the Juan Seguin School zone. I told him that it was wrong and he was discriminating against my son. I told him that I needed the letter so that I could take him to federal court to sue him and Seguin ISD. He became alarmed and said that he did not want any trouble. He told me to give him sometime to speak to the school board members about the matter. I told him to do what he needed to do, but if my son was not allowed to transfer, I was going to take him to court.

After several days he called me at work in San Antonio and asked me to come by his office. When I arrived, I went to his office and he told me he had spoken to the school board members and they agreed that my son could attend Weinert. I said thank you. As

I was leaving, the superintendent said that he did not appreciate that I had threatened him. I responded by telling him that I did not threaten him with any bodily harm. I threatened him because of the district's racist policies and that was no threat. When he realized that I was angry, he told me okay, we do not want any trouble, and I replied neither do I, and I left. A middle school in Seguin ISD was named after Mr. Briesemeister.

Some parents of children that were to enroll at Juan Seguin found out that I had gotten a transfer from Juan Seguin to Weinert Elementary. One day I received a call from Edward Espinoza who was my wife's cousin's husband. He said he knew of my son's transfer and asked me if he and five other parents could come to talk to me about it. I said sure to come and talk about it. Edward was an Army veteran from the Korean War. He had been wounded in Korea and had been highly decorated for valor. Edward had learned how to fly a small airplane with training provided by the GI Bill.

One day Edward and four men and a woman come to my house to see me about their children's school situation. I remember the names of two of the other men, they were Vincent Medina and José Gallegos; two other men whose names I do not remember and a woman whose name I don't remember either. They were all Mexican-American. First they wanted to know how I got the transfer for my son. I told them I had gotten approval by the superintendent after I threatened to take him to court for discrimination. They said they had all gone to see the superintendent and had also gone before the school board, but they all had denied them the transfers. Then they asked me if I could help them, and be the spoke person of the group, to which I agreed.

Two weeks before our meeting at home we went before the Seguin ISD School Board to request that their children be allowed to transfer. Again the board said no. At the meeting Robert Koennecke, the Board President, asked what was it that the people wanted. I told him we don't want a thing except to be treated fairly and equally, and with that we left the meeting.

I called a meeting of the parents the following week and told them of some new recommendations that I wanted to make. I told them that we should make this a public issue, go to the news media and tell them what is happening after we went public. Anglos, Blacks and Mexican-Americans became highly concerned about what was happening, it brought to light the ugly and discriminatory practice and policies of Seguin ISD. My next recommendation was to get legal advice and find out what we needed to do to sue the district in federal court for discrimination.

I said I would contact two attorney friends of mine and see what they would recommend. I contacted them. One was Bob Vale, who was a state senator and the other was John Alaniz who was a state representative. We met with them and told them the situation and asked what would they would recommend to solve the problem. They both agreed that taking them to federal court would not be prudent, because at that time there were really no federal laws that could force Seguin ISD to do what we wanted. They recommended to take the case to the Texas Commission of Education. Commissioner Edgar was the head of the Texas Education Agency which had certain jurisdiction over all the schools in Texas. The agency was under the supervision of the Texas Board of Education. Vale and Alaniz agreed to take the case for a very nominal fee.

On the day of the scheduled meeting about twenty of us went to Austin as witnesses and/or plaintiffs. The school district sent several staff members including James Guttery who was principal of the school. Our group had extensive information and documentation to prove our case. Vale and Alaniz were highly assertive and extensively questioned James Guttery and other district officers. They also questioned many of us as witnesses or plaintiffs. After half a day of meeting and testimony, Commissioner Edgar dismissed the meeting and advised everyone that he would render a decision in two weeks and inform both parties of his decision by letter. About three weeks we received Commissioner Edgar's decision in a letter written by the state attorney and informed us that he found our group to have very valid concern and ruled in our favor. Secondly, other recommendations for Seguin were to initiate a desegregating of all schools including the schools for the Blacks, who were all totally segregated. The order from Commissioner Edgar also prescribed that the district avoid gerrymandering to keep students segregated in any school. The order also triggered the integration of all schools in Seguin ISD. This was 1963.

My involvement in the school segregation was the most traumatic situation I have ever been involved Seguin. First it was the public criticism by many Anglos against me and the other parents for protesting the segregation of Seguin ISD. Secondly, it was the number of things I personally received by phone since I was the spokesperson for the group. Of course all the threats were anonymous. People would tell me what some Anglos were saying against me. There was only one occasion where I could prove that someone was saying derogatory things about me.

My wife Velia was working with the school as an aide for the migrant program. This included making home visitation. One afternoon she was visiting a parent and she and the lady were outside the house when an insurance agent came by to collect the insurance monthly premium. According to my wife, he asked her what she thought of that guy Sam Flores who was causing all the trouble for the school. He also commented and told her that I was a no good rebel, nuisance and someone should run him out of town. He continued to say a lot of ugly things about me.

Finally my wife asked him how he could say all that against me. My wife told him that she was my wife and what he was saying was not true. The man was startled and left. When I came from work my wife told me what the man had said she also told me who the man was. I called the man by phone and told him what my wife had said. I told him I am considering suing you and your insurance company for slander and defamation of character. I said I am not an elected official that you can say many things about without being held accountable. The man became alarmed and said that he was very sorry and apologized for what he said. He said that he wanted to come to my house and apologize to me personally. He came to my house almost in tears and pleaded with me not to sue him and the insurance company he worked for. I said I wouldn't sue him and I would accept his apology. I did advise him to refrain from talking about me. He invited me to his church I declined to accept. After that we became good friends until this day, when I see him he's very cordial and attentive.

My work at Harlandale High School continued well and I am in good standing. I had good support with everyone at school. I was in charge of the facilities, all school activities, and a portion of the students discipline problem. Discipline referrals were handled by the four vice-principals, Harlandale High School was a school in good standing. We had a group of excellent teachers and other staff members. We had organized all types of student participation. Our students were very competitive in athletics and many extra-curricular activities allowed by the university interscholastic league under the supervision and sponsorship of the Texas Education Agency.

After the school's principal died around 1966 the principal was Dr. Bowden who had been principal for many years at Harlandale High School. He was the first principal in San Antonio to hold a doctor's degree, when he died the school board appointed Douglas Sheedy as the new principal. Mr. Sheedy was there several years and left to be superintendent at Marble Falls, Texas. When he left in 1970 the school board appointed Frank Nestra as principal. Frank had graduated from Harlandale and had been an outstanding football player. In 1973 Frank came to my office and said Sam I can't handle this job much longer I can't stand it. I am going to ask the superintendent to assign me to an elementary school. I agreed with Frank that the principal's job was demanding. What triggered Frank's decision was that one day while he was away at a meeting unknown to anyone, the teacher organizations met in what they called the Faculty Senate. Many of the teachers were dissatisfied with Frank's leadership. In those days teacher organizations like the senate were prohibited. The teachers wanted a voice in all school matters.

The following year the superintendent appointed Frank as principal at Flanders Elementary School. Before the end of the year and before Frank transferred, Mr. Charles Boggess, the superintendent told me that Frank was leaving and wanted me to consider being principal at Harlandale High School. I was highly surprised and thanked him and told him that I wanted to consult with my wife. Mr. Boggess added that if I were to accept the job I would have to move to San Antonio. I got home and discussed the offer with my wife. Of course both of us were extremely happy for the superintendent's consideration. My wife and I decided to go to San Antonio and look at the city and look at homes and see how our children would handle going to school. My oldest son Cesar was fourteen years old. Samuel was twelve and Leticia was ten.

After visiting San Antonio we decided that it would be a very traumatic experience for our children to live there and we decided to decline the offer for this position. Several days later I went to Mr. Boggess' office and explained to him that my wife and I had discussed and reviewed the offer and because we felt it was not the best thing for our children that I would not accept the position. Mr. Boggess said he was sorry to hear that. Then he told me that he had 2,000 other teachers in the district and I was the only one he trusted with managing the high school. He said with my permission he would go to the school board and request that the board consider giving me a waiver for the policy the district required, which stated that one should live in the San Antonio area. The board heard his request and agreed that I could remain in Seguin and be principal at Harlandale High School. I thanked Mr. Boggess I had become the first Mexican-American principal at Harlandale High School. I thanked God for his help.

In 1962 I had run for a position on the Seguin ISD School Board. To my knowledge, no Hispanic had ever attempted for a seat on the school board. Winning a position and getting elected especially for a minority was very difficult. The election was at large there were no single member districts. Before I filed for a position on the school board I did a lot of planning and organizing. I had a large committee composed by all Hispanics that were helping in the campaign.

On elections day, the return came in and I had lost by eleven votes to Tom Crump who was a wealthy Anglo that owned a lumber yard in Seguin. Crump was board president for many years and a boys gymnasium at Seguin High School campus bears his name. In 1963 I organized a committee of all Hispanics. It was to get the minorities involved in civic and political affairs. I was also geared to get students to stay enrolled in school and complete their education. We were involved in many other areas like getting people to vote and to register to vote. There were many huge problems for Hispanics, such as housing, getting better jobs, etc. While we were organizing the council for Civic Betterment many Anglos in Seguin were angered and afraid that we were out to take over the City of Seguin. During that same time in Crystal City Hispanics were gaining several elected positions previously ocuppied only by Anglos. The whole effort was lead by José Ángel Gutiérrez. We finally convinced most of the citizens that our purpose was to improve the quality of life for the Mexican-American citizens of Seguin. The committee efforts were very successful.

In 1963 a friend of mine, Dr. Roger Bell, came to my home and told me that he needed my help. He wanted to organize a federal program to help the poor, "The War on Poverty" under President Lyndon B. Johnson. I read most of the information he had on the program and I told him that I would help him. I told him that according to the information we would need the support and the signature of the Mayor of Seguin and the Guadalupe County Judge. Dr. Bell said he would get the needed signatures. A week later he came again and said he had the mayor's and county judges' signature. Dr. Bell took out a long piece of paper, it was paper from a brown lunch bag. He gave it to me and on that brown page he had the mayor and county judges' signatures. With that we proceeded to organize the Community Council and applied for the federal funding to organize the organization. It took long before we got approved to organize the council it was required that a board of offices had to be organized to run the program. During the first organized meeting many of the city and county citizens and elected officials including Senator John Traeger attended. Dr. Bell stood up and said he was going to be president and that I would be vice-president of the group. I stopped Mr. Bell and told him that we could not do that, members had to be elected by the board of the community council, where they would elect the officers and the executive officer. The board was organized and elected. They named Louis Saegert, a lawyer and city attorney, to be the first president. The Guadalupe County Community Council still is functioning but now situated in Seguin has emerged as a community council for eleven counties with offices in Seguin.

I assumed the principal position of Harlandale High School. The school had an enrollment of 2,800 students. It was a small campus, but we managed to do well with what we had. The school had a good dedicated group of administrators, teachers, and staff. We had a good student body and there were some concerns affecting most schools in the nation. First it was during the Vietnam War, we had a small group of students that organized demonstrations against Vietnam; it was also a source on campus for an underground newspaper. The major problem were the boys starting to wear long hair and girls starting to wear pants, and as I said before, there was the problem of drugs showing up on campus.

In Seguin, a good number of us became more involved in bringing awareness to minorities about getting involved. We lead the effort of a group of about twelve of us. The person leading the effort was Jim Bode. Jim was an Anglo teacher who had great desire to see improvement and equality. There was a man named Roger and his wife. Roger was a law student who later became a lawyer. They were all Anglos. This was a small group of Blacks including Earl Redix, John Randle, Mr. and Mrs. Davies, and me, the only Hispanic.

Jim Bodie was the moving force of this effort. We registered many people to vote. We brought out awareness to the minorities of the problem we were facing. This small group was aggressive and assertive and was doing very well within the law to improve things. We saw the great injustice of discrimination and we organized a group named the Seguin Bi-Racial Committee. We took our concern to the media and to the public and looked for ways to improve things. One of the first things we addressed with the great injustices to the Blacks. One concern was that Blacks could not use public restaurants. It they needed something from a restaurant they had to go to the kitchen to get what they wanted and leave. I still get angry when I think of this. We developed a plan where several of us, including Jim Bode and I would go to a restaurant with some of our Black friends, sit down and order something to eat.

The first place we went was called the King Bee on Kingsbury Street which is now Davila's BBQ. We ordered, everyone was served and we were highly elated. We went to four other Seguin eating establishments and again nothing happened. In the many places that we went to, we did face one minor problem. We went to a restaurant on West Kingsbury Street where Cristina's Mexican was recently located. We all ordered something to eat and everyone was served except Jim Bode, this was done to spite Jim because he was white. Jim could care less. He was glad that all Blacks had been served. James Bode later moved to San Antonio where he continued teaching and became involved in public affairs. Because of his good work he was appointed as a member of the Texas Democratic National Committee. In politics this is a high position. He died about eight years later. Some people who worked with him wanted to honor him for his work. They proposed that a park be named in his honor. The recommendation was approved and today the James Bode Park in San Antonio is a symbol of his dedication and concern for people.

In 1964 I decided to run for the Seguin City Council Ward I. Manuel Castilla was the first Hispanic to serve on the Seguin City Council. Manuel was a WWII veteran. He was a dedicated worker for helping people. After serving his first two years he was defeated by August Kutac. I ran against Kutac, again with a well organized campaign and funding, I defeated Kutac by a margin of two to one. For many years Manuel and I, and now many others, were working for the Community Betterment. When Manuel died I contacted his wife Estella to get her approval to develop a city park and name it after Manuel. She agreed and today the Manuel Castilla Park on the north side of town is a symbol of his dedication and service to the people of Seguin.

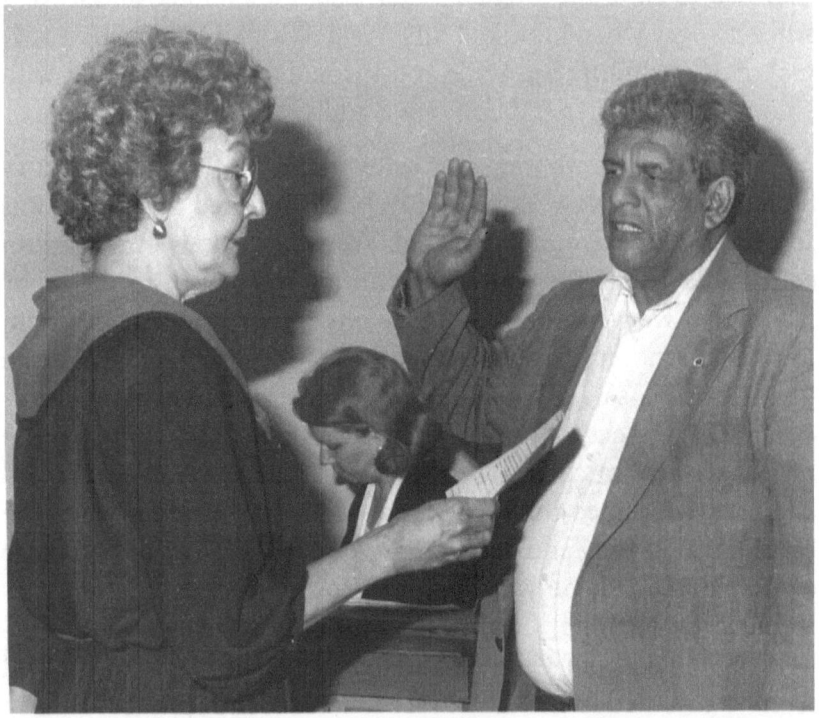

Mayor Betty Jean Jones administering the oath of office to councilman Sam Flores.

In 1975 after I had been principal of Harlandale High School. I was elected by the membership to be president of the Harlandale Administration Association. This involved representing all the district administrations staff. We were a unit of the Texas State Teachers Association. We worked for improvement and better salaries for teachers. I went to Austin several times to lobby for the legislation for better benefits for teachers.

At Harlandale High School I was concerned about the demand of the job for all, but more specifically for the principal and the four vice-principals. One of the major problems was that we had an open campus that meant that at noon all the students were allowed to go home for lunch. Many students walked home for lunch. Many students and others had cars and left with them. Some students ate in the cafeteria. The major problem was that during the lunch period one had fights happening off campus, and then at lunch also students from other schools would come to visit with some of our students. We had two lunch periods and a vice-principal or principal had duty in front of the building. This period reminded me of a carnival type of entertainment. Sometimes we had student fights. It was very traumatic for us pulling this duty.

One day after a hectic work day, I decided that I would contact the superintendent to give me the authority to close the campus and do away with the open campus. I went and told Mr. Boggess what I wanted to do. He said the school should have done away with the open campus, but they were afraid to do so. He said you have my permission but you are going to have a student revolt. About a week after speaking to Mr. Boggess I notified all the school personnel, the students and parents that on a certain day the school campus would be closed at noon, only students that worked or had school permissions were allowed to leave. Surprisingly the campus plan was implemented without a problem.

The school moved forward swiftly with teachers and students doing their best to have the best learning environments. My greatest pleasure was the time our students graduated. It was a great pleasure seeing the hundreds of students and thousands of their parents, participating in their beautiful ceremonies. Most of our graduation ceremonies were in San Antonio at the Municipal

Auditorium. At the graduation ceremonies I gave my principal's address in both English and Spanish.

In Seguin in the early 1970's the Mexican-American citizens were getting more involved in civic affairs. Several major groups, LULAC, The American GI Forum, and the Council for Civic Betterment were constantly encouraging people to get involved in the schools, in the city, the county and the federal government. The Hispanic Community became more knowledgeable of its rights and responsibilities as citizens took legal steps through many organizations like LULAC, The American GI Forum, the NAACP, and started asking for the City of Seguin, Seguin ISD and Guadalupe County to organize into single member districts. This would allow minorities an opportunity to be elected to elective offices. Seguin ISD is now organized in three minority districts giving the opportunity for three minority individuals to be elected to the seven member school board.

The Seguin City Council was sued and came up with five minority districts out of eight. Only the mayor and the city secretary run at-large. Presently, elected to the five minority districts are Mary Louise Gonzales, Manuel Cevallos, Tomás V. Castellón Jr., Nick Carrillo and Carlos Medrano. Thalia Patlán Stautzenberger, the wife of the former Mayor Mark Stautzenberger is the current city secretary. She ran at-large. She is my niece. Kathy Contreras was the first Hispanic city secretary elected at-large in Seguin. She was the city secretary but was defeated by Thalia.

In my opinion, many good changes have occurred socially, civically, politically and economically. The more people interested in community betterment, the better community we will have.

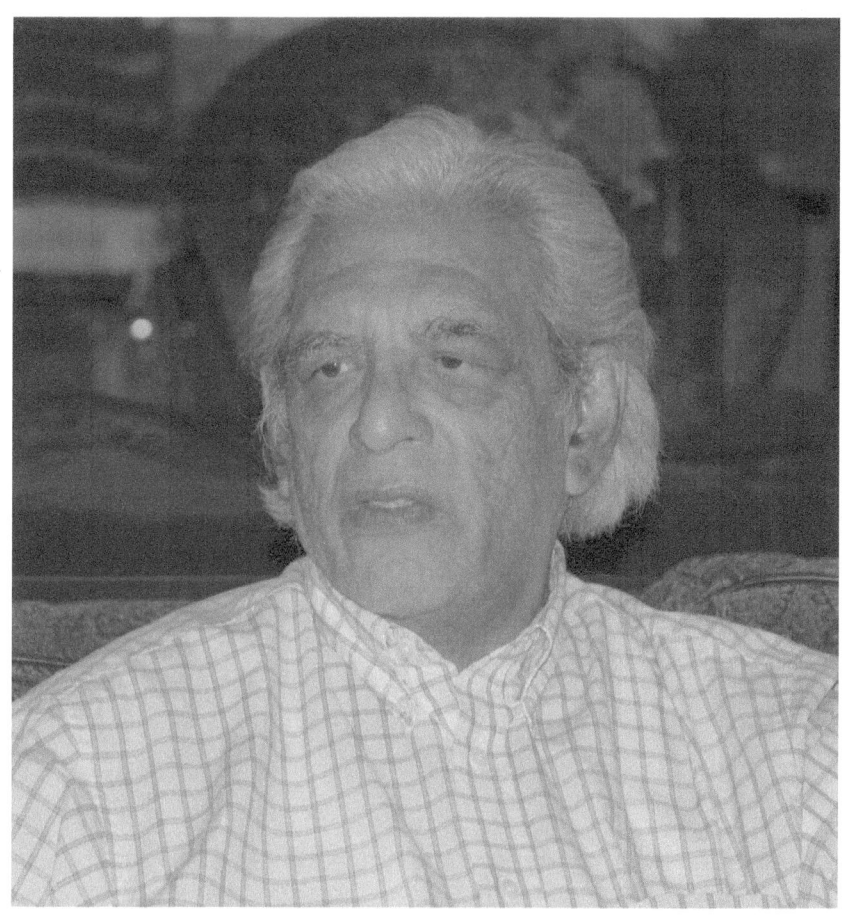

Mr. Flores at his home during the interview by Dr. González, 2010.

Community Projects

These are some of the projects in which Mr. Flores was involved in one way or another:

Affirmative Action Ordinance

Bond issue for Fire Station on E. Kingsbury and N. 123 Bypass

Boys Club

Bridge Saunders St.

City – Single Member Districts

City Council

Community Council of South Central Texas

Council for Civic Betterment

Disable American Veterans Office on Vaughn St.

Employment Recommendations

Food Stamp Program

Gangs (assisted in truce in 1990's)

Hospital

Housing

Juan Seguin Statue (spearheaded)

Juvenile Retention Center

King Street

Kingsbury St. and Eight St. Traffic Light

Landscape 123 Bypass

Library

Life Gate School Street Crossing

Manuel Castilla Park

Post office

Railroad traffic light at Guadalupe St.

Rodriguez School

School – Single Member Districts

School Segregation

Sebastopol

Seguin Bi-Racial Committee

Seguin Public Education Forum

Street Improvements

Street Lighting

Texas Human Relations Commission (appointment)

Texas State Health Clinic

TLU – Mexican-American Studies

Tyson Poultry Plant (odor issue and limited drainage)

Veteran's Clinic

Veteran's Monument (served on board)

Voting Registration

W. New Braunfels St. (rebuilt)

Walnut Springs Creek Project

Water Contract

Water Tank on E. Kingsbury Logo

SWEET DREAMS

Eulogy for Uncle Sam Flores

by Niece Thalia Patlán Stautzenberger

Today we say good-bye to my Uncle Sam.

All of you who love him, know him as Father, Husband, Uncle, Grandfather, Great-Grandfather or as his brothers and sisters affectionately call him "Sambito". Those of you in the community know him as colleague, educator, mentor and friend.

Hoy le decimos adiós a mi Tío Samuel. Todos los que lo aman lo conocen como padre, marido, tío, abuelo, bisabuelo o como sus hermanos cariñosamente lo llaman "Sambito". Y los de la comunidad lo conocen como colaborador, educador, mentor y amigo.

As a child growing up my first memories of my uncle... I remember him tall, strong and handsome with a loving heart. I can picture him singing coritos in church, his humorous quips, that little grin and the twinkle in his eye. He was always there providing a gentle hand and unconditional love for his family. He was a Christian man who loved his God.

De niña los primeros recuerdos de mi tío... era alto, fuerte, guapo y con un corazón lleno de amor. Mis memorias me llevan a un tiempo cuando él cantaba coritos en la iglesia, recuerdo sus chistes y bromas y recuerdo su sonrisa. Siempre se prestaba de una manera bondadosa y con un amor sin condiciones para su familia. Era un hombre cristiano que siempre amaba a su DIOS.

Always deep in thought, he felt profoundly compelled to make the world in which he lived better for all. As a man of conviction and passion, he approached each day with a drive and fervor to alleviate the affliction and to strive to fill the needs of the people of this community which he loved.

Siempre profundamente en pensamiento, se sentía obligado para hacer del mundo en el cual vivió un mejor lugar para todos. Como hombre de convicción, recibió cada día con un fervor para aliviar la aflicción y para esforzarse a llenar las necesidades de la gente de esta comunidad que él amó.

We will remember him as the protector who PERSEVERED... for those who were the silent few. He was a man with a quest filled with courage and bravery to see a reality for those in need: the citizen denied his rights, the young child whose parents yearned for an education, the youth who wished for a place to play and learn, the veteran seeking medical assistance or the elderly or the poor seeking shelter and those who sought to improve the quality of life in our community.

Lo recordamos como el protector que PERSEVERÓ para los que no tenían voz. Él era un hombre con una búsqueda llena de valor de ver las aspiraciones hechas realidad para todos los que pasaban alguna necesidad: el ciudadano negado de sus derechos, el niño cuyos padres anhelaron una educación, el joven que deseaba un lugar donde jugar y aprender, el veterano que buscaba asistencia médica, los ancianos o pobres buscando refugio, y todos los que intentaron mejorar la calidad de vida en nuestra comunidad.

As Robert Frost penned in his poem THE ROAD NOT TAKEN

"Two roads diverged in a yellow wood...

And I took the one less traveled by,

And that has made all the difference."

Uncle Sam chose the road less traveled because of his compassion for his fellow man... he did so to give a voice to those who had no voice…

Como dice el poeta Roberto Frost en su poema EL CAMINO NO TOMADO

Describe que al llegar a un bosque uno encuentra dos caminos, pero él eligió tomar el camino menos viajado. Y esa fue la diferencia… mi tío Samuel optó por el camino menos viajado debido a su compasión por su prójimo, lo hizo para dar una voz a los que no tenían ninguna voz…

Con la partida de nuestro querido Tío Samuel se termina una crónica en los acontecimientos de la vida, pero la vida es como un collar de perlas… historias tejidas…

Debemos reflejar sobre su vida, su historia y edificar sobre la fundación que él construyó. Si hemos aprendido y podemos reflejar solamente lo que él representaba… entonces nosotros lo honramos para siempre.

Lo recordaremos por su herencia de compasión y su generoso corazón.

DULCES SUEÑOS, TÍO SAMUEL…

The passing of our beloved Uncle Sam ends one chronicle in life's events... but

Life is like a string of pearls… stories woven together…

We must reflect upon his life, his story and build upon the foundation which he has laid. If we who have stood on his shoulders can only mirror what he stood for… then we will honor him for always.

We will remember him for his legacy of compassion and his giving heart.

SWEET DREAMS, UNCLE SAM…